THE WASHINGTON PAPERS
Volume IV

40: Culture and Information: Two Foreign Policy Functions

Terry L. Deibel
Walter R. Roberts

THE CENTER FOR STRATEGIC AND INTERNATIONAL STUDIES
Georgetown University, Washington, D.C.

SAGE PUBLICATIONS
Beverly Hills / London

For information address:

SAGE PUBLICATIONS, INC.
275 South Beverly Drive
Beverly Hills, California 90212

SAGE PUBLICATIONS LTD
St George's House / 44 Hatton Garden
London EC1N 8ER

International Standard Book Number 0-8039-0789-3

Library of Congress Catalog Card No. 76-50436

SECOND PRINTING

*When citing a Washington Paper, please use the proper form. Remember to cite
the series title and include the paper number. One of the two following formats
can be adapted (depending on the style manual used):*

(1) HASSNER, P. (1973) "Europe in the Age of Negotiation." The Washington
Papers, I, 8. Beverly Hills and London: Sage Pubns.

OR

(2) Hassner, Pierre. 1973. *Europe in the Age of Negotiation*. The Washington
Papers, vol. 1, no. 8. Beverly Hills and London: Sage Publications.

CONTENTS

Foreword by Frank Stanton   5

Authors' Preface   7

I. Information and Culture in Modern
    International Affairs   11

II. The Origins of Political and Cultural
    Propaganda   17

III. The Programs   22

IV. Policy Information and Cultural Communications—
    Two Different Foreign Policy Functions   56

Notes   62

References   62

0886500

FOREWORD

During my chairmanship of the U.S. Advisory Commission on Information, I became acutely aware of two problems which face the American international information and cultural effort:

(1) Although the Department of State has nominal responsibility for articulating policies overseas, this responsibility is in fact carried out by the largely independent United States Information Agency;

(2) The Voice of America, as the government's official radio, is at times unable to function with sufficient latitude as an objective disseminator of news and views.

In retrospect, many of the problems which confronted the Advisory Commission during the years I was its chairman revolved around these two conceptual contradictions. Indeed, I have observed on more than one occasion that no Secretary of State should permit another agency, even one receiving "policy input" from the Department of State, to speak for the United States government overseas. I have also believed that there is an inherent inconsistency in considering the Voice of America the "official" radio and at the same time asking it to present "accurate, objective, and comprehensive news."

In the early 1970s, when important voices in and out of government were raising thoughtful questions about the adequacy of U.S. informational and cultural efforts overseas, I was asked to chair a private panel of distinguished Americans knowledgeable in the fields of international relations and communications to look into the organizational structure. It was no surprise to find the same problems that I had encountered during my years with the Advisory Commission coming up again. Nor was it a great surprise that my fellow panelists, almost unanimously, reached the same conclusions as I had.

Two former government officers assisted our panel in its task: a senior officer who had served both in the United States and overseas and who had retired from the highest career position in USIA, and a junior officer who had been with the Office of Management and Budget. Walter Roberts and Terry Deibel have now collaborated in a study which provides a significant adjunct to the report and recommendations submitted by our panel. They have found that other countries with longer experience in international information and cultural affairs have organized themselves along lines that differ from those of the United States. In doing so, these countries have avoided the two problem areas which plague U.S. programs. Thus, in other countries the information effort—that is, the articulation of policy—is firmly lodged in the Foreign Office (in Germany in the Chancellery). The international radio service, on the other hand, is a step removed from government: witness the British Broadcasting Corporation, the Canadian Broadcasting Corporation, Deutsche Welle, and so forth. At the same time, the cultural effort—that is, the presentation of national values and societies—is lodged in semi-governmental organizations such as the British Council, the Alliance Francaise, the Goethe Houses, or the Japan Foundation.

Roberts and Deibel have made a substantial contribution by using the experience of other countries to point conclusively to logical ways of organizing the information and cultural activities. They argue persuasively that the time has come for the United States to work out its own solution along similar lines.

Frank Stanton
Chairman, U.S. Advisory Commission
on Information (1964-1973)
Former President, CBS

Authors' Preface

From April 1974 to March 1975, the authors had the distinct pleasure of serving a study panel on international information, education, and cultural relations at Georgetown University's Center for Strategic and International Studies. That panel, chaired by Dr. Frank Stanton and composed of more than a score of prominent experts in the fields of international communications, education, and diplomacy, was primarily concerned with the study of the U.S. government's organization for the conduct of international information and cultural programs. It recommended a thoroughgoing reorganization of the United States Information Agency and the Bureau of Educational and Cultural Affairs of the State Department, separating the articulation and defense of U.S. foreign policy (to be done by State) from the portrayal of American society overseas (to be handled by a new autonomous Information and Cultural Affairs Agency), and establishing the Voice of America as a separate federal agency under a Board of Directors (Panel on International Information, Education, and Cultural Relations, 1975). These recommendations were adopted by the Murphy Commission on the Organization of the Government for the Conduct of Foreign Policy (1975), and broadly supported by a later study of the Congressional Research Service (1975).

They await consideration by a new administration as it sorts out proposals for reorganizing the international affairs sector of the Executive branch.

At the time the Stanton Panel was constituted, one of its funding sources also commissioned an empirical study by the C.S.I.S. of other governments' information and cultural programs in the United States. The authors were happy to undertake this task, as it had become apparent in the course of the Stanton Panel's investigation that in several respects other governments' programs show wide variations from the American pattern. While decisions about American institutions should certainly be made with domestic factors primarily in view, we believed that an examination of the information and cultural efforts of foreign governments (some of which have had longer experiences than the United States) might lend some perspective to the reorganization process. We thus undertook the study of other governments' information and cultural programs in the United States with the explicit intention of comparing them, not only to each other, but also to the programs of the American government.

It was, of course, impossible to undertake the study of all foreign programs here. In limiting the scope of this study, the authors felt it would be particularly interesting to focus on the programs of other industrialized countries in the United States, and reciprocally on the programs of the United States in those countries. In this way, we would have a set of countries that were comparable both in the resource base from which they operated and from the point of view of the environment they were attempting to influence.

We therefore picked the four industrial countries of France, the Federal Republic of Germany, the United Kingdom, and Japan as our objects of investigation. All are countries allied with the United States and sharing to a large extent the same foreign policy goals. The Soviet Union, although clearly of interest, did not fit with this group and was eliminated from our study. We have also ignored the programs of the developing world, feeling that their very special problems demand consideration in a separate project beyond the limits of our resources.

A word should be added about research techniques. We did not set out to produce a scholarly and theoretical analysis of these programs, nor did we feel it necessary to analyze every pamphlet, book, and video tape they produced. What was called for, we felt, was a distinctly practical look at the overall thrust of the programs with particular emphasis on the way practitioners in the field viewed them. We thus set out to do an extensive series of interviews with the information and cultural officers of the four embassies here in Washington, D.C. Their frank comments, absolutely essential to our inquiry, were gathered under the promise of confidentiality. As a result it is possible by way of attribution only for us to thank them for their efforts and assure them that without their cooperation the current study would have been impossible.

What has resulted from our efforts is really a two-dimensional work. First, it is a broad look at the information and cultural programs of five major industrial countries in other industrial countries, as viewed through the eyes of the people who manage them. Second, it is a comparative critical analysis that attempts to draw appropriate conclusions from the surprising fact that the countries surveyed conduct very similar programs in very different ways. Since we write from the perspective of Americans, most of our conclusions are directed at the American government's programs. Those from other countries may find other equally interesting results here from their own perspective.

The authors would like to acknowledge not only the generous assistance of the Lilly Endowment and the Ford Foundation, but also the staff of the Center for Strategic and International Studies for their capable and efficient support. We are, of course, enormously indebted to the information and cultural officers of the four foreign countries surveyed and of the United States Information Agency and the Bureau of Educational and Cultural Affairs at the Department of State for giving generously of their time and knowledge in the course of our research. Responsibility for what has been done with the information they furnished remains, as it should, with us.

Terry L. Deibel
Walter R. Roberts

September 1976

I. INFORMATION AND CULTURE IN MODERN INTERNATIONAL AFFAIRS

Information and culture are two terms which have had many interpretations, particularly when applied to foreign affairs. While it is very clear that these two terms are not mutually exclusive—one can inform about culture—it appears to be generally accepted in the area of international affairs that information connotes the one-sided advocacy of a point of view while culture signifies the furthering of mutual understanding.

The international information and cultural programs about to be analyzed took shape for the most part in the 30 years since the Second World War. Some of them have changed very little over that period of time, in spite of dramatic changes in the international environment to which they must address themselves. In fact, the world situation today is one in which information and cultural programs are both more important and far more difficult than ever before. Surprisingly enough, it is often the very same world conditions that contribute both to the importance and to the difficulty.

Take, for example, one of the extraordinary trends of recent times, namely, the worldwide decrease in the number of democratic governments in favor of dictatorships of the right or left. When democratic governmental forms disappear, so too does the freedom of expression of the media so essential for carrying on government communications programs. The result is that conditions of access become more and more restricted worldwide, and the tools available to the foreign propagandist become fewer and fewer. Yet, at the same time, the very lack of contact of closed societies with the rest of the world makes it doubly important for information and cultural programs to succeed in breaking down barriers to the flow of information. Thus, in terms of target environments, it is just where these programs have least chance of effectiveness that they are most needed.

A second factor that must be considered is the drastic change in the global political climate signified by the much-maligned word détente. Whether one sees in détente a genuine reconciliation of interests or merely a continuation of the East-West struggle by other means, it is clear that, in the perceptions of most governments, the Cold War as we knew it is over. With it has disappeared the intense commitment to ideological struggle that provided so much of the motivation for the propaganda "war for men's minds" that characterized the era of Truman, Dulles, and even Kennedy. And yet détente provides both new opportunities and new rationale for information and cultural programs. On the one hand, there are new openings between East and West for the flow of information, as codified in the accord signed at Helsinki last year. On the other hand, there is in détente an implied limitation on other, more abrasive weapons in the East-West confrontation that make information and cultural programs all the more important among those means that are left. Again, difficulty and necessity escalate hand in hand.

A third factor complicating the modern environment for information and cultural programs is the growing interdependence of the world and the awesome problems associated with it. Alongside the traditional interests that divide East from West and South from North are the problems that unite our stakes in the future: environmental pollution, world needs for food, ocean resources management, nuclear control, energy conservation, and so forth. Interdependence has turned what were once purely national problems into international concerns, and in so doing has brought world affairs into contact with the ordinary citizen in ways never before experienced. For these reasons, all nations find it more than ever necessary to explain and attempt to justify their policies to the common man overseas; because the consequences of their decisions are felt beyond their borders, all governments bear some responsibility to an international constituency. And yet the personal impact of the problems of interdependence creates new difficulties for information and cultural programs in that the immediate, personal interests of the target audiences may be hurt by the policies propaganda seeks to defend. Just at the time when the national policies of each state need more than ever to be accepted by others it is more than ever difficult to secure that acceptance.

Fourth in this catalogue of hostile yet encouraging influences are recent innovations in the technology of communications. Such devices as videotape recording, the new generation of higher-power radio transmitters, and the spread of the transistorized shortwave receiver have made it possible to reach those formerly beyond the range of the foreign propagandist. In so doing, however, these methods have encouraged a new era of competition between nations in communications, making it increasingly difficult for any one protagonist to get his message across. Moreover, the communications explosion usually signals the growth of local media, too, thus doubly increasing the competition for the foreign propagandist.

On top of all these difficulties there is one final adverse factor in today's information and cultural environment that must be mentioned, namely, the effect of inflation and competing domestic programs on each government's limited budget. When resources are scarce, international information and cultural activities are easy to cut. Except for those sent overseas to learn or teach, these activities provide no direct benefit to the citizen. Even among indirect benefits in the foreign affairs field these programs offer nothing as tangible as treaties, economic agreements, or defense hardware to reassure the taxpayer that his funds are being well spent. They are one step removed from such concrete achievements, being in the nature of support for foreign policy, and in addition they are notoriously hard to evaluate. They deal with the subtle forming of ideas, with the climate within which policy is conducted, an area little amenable to cost-benefit analysis.

As the result of an environment compounded of all these factors, then, governments engaging in information and cultural work today are faced with a particular need to know what they are about. That is no easy task. The purposes of information and cultural programs are traditionally defined in extremely general and often vague terms, such as "building mutual understanding" or "influencing foreign public attitudes." The programs themselves are composed of an incredible variety of activities, running the gamut from pamphlet publication to cultural exchanges to international radio broadcasting. Under these circumstances a conscious effort must be made to set purposes firmly and relate activities to them.

Perhaps the first question to be asked and answered is whether information and cultural programs are part of one program serving a single function or whether they are in some way conceptually and operationally distinct. In this regard it is worth noting that no one has yet discovered an English-language phrase that adequately covers the programs taken together. The term "public diplomacy" is used by some, but that conjures up a mental image of diplomats engaged in traditional negotiations under the glare of publicity. That certainly is not what public diplomacy is all about. "Government-to-people programs" is perhaps a better defintion of the reality here, since what distinguishes information and cultural programs from traditional diplomacy is that they involve governments' communications with the people of other countries rather than with their foreign offices. But even here the term is not comprehensive, since many activities on the cultural side are really people-to-people activities with the government acting as catalyst and facilitator.

In fact, there is no single term that adequately describes all these activities. Yet the effort to find such a term and the failure to do so both contain important clues to clear thinking on the subject. The activities generally subsumed under the label public diplomacy do have several things in common. In the first place, they are all communications programs; in many cases, they use the same media to reach people overseas. They thus all deal in the psychology of alien societies, with the basic problem of changing the attitudes of people in foreign cultures. Also, they are all designed to support foreign policy. But beneath these superficial similarities there are more important differences that can lead the theoretician to confusion and the practitioner to failure if he fails to recognize them.

For example, there has been for the last decade or more in the United States an ongoing debate between two general conceptions of what a so-called "public diplomacy" program ought to be like. Though the participants are talking about the same set of activities, they are so far apart on purpose and methods of execution that they seem to be (and in fact are) talking about two very different kinds of programs. Their views are worth looking at in some detail, because they point to the real functions which these programs should address.

For want of a better term we might label these general schools of thought, after William James (1955), as the tough- and tender-minded. The tough-minded argue that the purpose of public diplomacy is to influence foreign attitudes in ways favorable to the image and policies of the nation. They accept, even glory in the use of the word propaganda to describe their work; only for such hard-nosed efforts, they assert, is it morally justifiable to commit public resources. The tough-minded tend to see public diplomacy as primarily an information rather than a cultural program, relying principally on the fast media (such as radio, TV, and newsprint) to carry hard political messages. Though most do not deny the necessity of a certain degree of balance and objectivity to a credible (and therefore effective) program, neither do they extol truth as the highest virtue. *Raison d'état* fills that role, and the tough-minded public diplomatist stands ready to push whatever line seems best calculated to advance the policy need of the moment.

Against this formidable portrait of ruthless realism stands the opposite school of the tender-minded. Taking infinite pains to show that their position is no less realistic or supportive of foreign policy than that of their tough-minded opponents, these people insist that information and cultural programs must bypass current foreign policy goals to concentrate on the highest long-range national objectives. In this view, changing foreign attitudes is a process to be measured in years, and the only feasible goal is to create a climate of mutual understanding in which the particulars of future national policies can be communicated abroad in a receptive atmosphere. Unlike their opponents, this school specifies the foreign policy goals that information and cultural programs should support: in particular, peace and cooperative solutions to the major problems of the world. The tender-minded thus tend to view public diplomacy as predominately a cultural effort, relying on slow media (such as films, exhibits, language instruction, academic and artistic exchanges) to convey broad-gauged messages about the lifestyle, mores, political and economic systems, and artistic genius of the nation. The emphasis is on truth, in the belief that over the long run such a program can only be effective if reasonably accurate.

Who is right? In fact, each correctly identifies an important function performed by public diplomacy.

First, all public diplomacy programs have a primary responsibility to *explain and defend government policies to foreign audiences.* This is a necessary role because so much of today's foreign policy depends at least partly upon popular acceptance for its support. It is not enough today simply for a government to explain its policy in private to other governments; the world expects to be informed if not consulted. This role as spokesman for governmental policies therefore must be performed by every government.

Alongside it, however, lies a second important function, that of *portraying the national society in toto to foreign audiences.* This is the "cultural" side of what is called public diplomacy, and the reasons behind it are much less well-defined than those behind the spokesman role. They may relate to long-range goals of peace through mutual understanding, to a historic respect for the opinions of mankind, or to the ongoing need of a nation to assert and in the process define its identity in the family of nations. The central point is that the vast majority of nations see the need for some projection of themselves as well as their policies, of society as well as government.

Public diplomacy, then, is essentially an artificial term. What we have instead are two quite different functions: that of policy articulation and advocacy (the "policy information" role), and that of portraying the national society overseas ("cultural communications" in its broadest sense).

The tough-minded referred to above are quite right in isolating the policy information function. Where they err is in demanding that all information and cultural programs support it. By the same token, the tender-minded above are quite right in championing cultural communications; where they err is to assume that the policy information function can be ignored. Both programs are needed, and the administration of each must be conducted in full knowledge of the other. But it is our primary thesis that the two must be kept administratively and organizationally separate if each is to fulfill its unique purpose.

The pages that follow will substantiate this thesis and in the process explain why such functional separation is essential to the integrity of a modern, governmental, overseas communications program. We begin with a historical look at how policy information and cultural communications originated, each in a very distinct and separate manner, in the diplomatic history of Europe and the United States. We will then proceed with an examination of the policy information and cultural communications programs of five industrial countries: France, West Germany, the United Kingdom, Japan, and the United States. In so doing we will attempt to isolate the objectives these very different programs try to serve, the themes and subjects they stress, the media used to carry those messages, and the organizational structures that the governments have felt most appropriate to their successful execution. The concluding chapter will sum up the empirical data in theoretical terms applicable to information and cultural programs in the 1970s and beyond.

II. THE ORIGINS OF POLITICAL AND CULTURAL PROPAGANDA

W hen we talk of international information and cultural programs we are addressing dimensions of diplomacy that have only in recent times been generally recognized as important. Nevertheless, history is full of examples of successful (and unsuccessful) undertakings of this kind. The idea of reaching the people of another country over the head of the indigenous government is as old as civilization itself. Had not the word propaganda acquired very odious connotations, it would still be used in international affairs. After all, it had very respectable origins; it was the Roman Catholic Church to which we owe the very word propaganda— *congregatio de propaganda fide*—the committee of cardinals established by Pope Gregory XV to propagate the faith around the world.

Much has been written about the origins of international propaganda.[1] Learned scholars have found it in the Old Testament and in Homer. But for our purposes, international propaganda came into its own in France in the seventeenth and eighteenth centuries. And history demonstrates a clear division of political from cultural propaganda, or, as we might put it, of policy information from cultural communications.

Let us start with the latter. It was cultural propaganda that carried French culture beyond France's borders. As early as 1689, a French college was founded in Prussia. Peter the Great of Russia employed a French architect to build a palace outside St. Petersburg and Frederick the Great ordered that French be spoken in the Court of Prussia. French replaced Latin as the language of diplomats.

During the French Revolution, political propaganda was used with fervor by the champions of the "new order." Robespierre said that "it is not for one people we are fighting but for the entire universe." France's neighbors became the target of French pamphlets and agents. Soon these neighbors rallied and organized a counterpropaganda of their own.

Political propaganda as practiced during the French Revolution found its most effective application over 100 years later in the aftermath of the communist takeover in Russia. Inasmuch as world revolution was a major goal of communism in general, the establishment of communism in one country, Russia, offered the opportunity to propagate this ideology from a secure base: as early as 1917, the wireless telegraph was employed by Moscow for political propaganda. The "proletarians" all over Europe were asked to rise against their bourgeois oppressors and to end World War I. During the peace negotiations with Germany at Brest-Litovsk, the Soviets transmitted the actual proceedings by wireless and appealed to German workers and soldiers over the head of the German government to go on strike and to refuse military service.

When in the succeeding years many governments sharply reacted to this kind of political propaganda, the Soviets created a buffer organization, the Comintern, which carried forward the political propaganda work, thus allowing the Soviet government to distance itself officially from such activities. Another device employed by the Soviets was to use cultural propaganda for political purposes. The propagation of Russian, that is, Soviet, culture abroad was (and still is today) effectively utilized as a part of political propaganda.

This was an idea foreign to those originators of cultural propaganda, the French. The desire to teach French to other people led in 1883 to the creation of the Alliance Francaise for the propagation of the French language in the colonies and in foreign lands. In 1900, a special section was established in the French Foreign Office to keep contact with and support private French schools and other French organizations abroad.

Germany became the first country to follow France in the area of cultural propaganda. Long before Germany became a unified country, the predecessor states propagated German culture abroad through schools, Protestant churches, and several kinds of institutes. An arts and science section was created in the German Foreign Office in 1896 and a schools section in 1906. Indeed, an exchange of American and German university professors began in 1905.

With the outbreak of the First World War, political propaganda pushed cultural propaganda into the background in France and Germany. Britain and the United States created governmental organizations whose purpose was political propaganda—to persuade neutral nations of the righteousness of the Allied cause and to lower the will to resist among citizens of the enemy countries.

At the end of the First World War, all political propaganda departments (except the Soviet Union's) were disbanded; the French and German governments, however, immediately resurrected their cultural efforts. The cultural departments in the two foreign offices were expanded. In Germany, the Goethe Institute was founded in 1932 to promote the teaching of German abroad.

When Hitler came to power in 1933, he did exactly the same thing that the Soviets had done earlier; he perverted cultural propaganda for political purposes.

For both the Soviets and the Nazis the medium of radio proved to be an excellent vehicle to propagate the state-directed mixture of politics and culture. Radio Moscow and Radio Berlin did not confine themselves to broadcasts in their own languages but added foreign languages to their schedules. Italy and Japan proceeded in similar fashion, and during the Spanish Civil War both sides used the medium of radio with great vigor.

Britain, which unlike France and Germany had never officially sponsored cultural propaganda and had abandoned political propaganda at the end of World War I, began to consider some activity in the cultural field in the mid-1930s in an effort to counter the Nazi propaganda campaign. A "British Council for Relations with other Countries" was founded in 1935 but received little in government funds and obtained its Royal Charter only in 1940, one year after the outbreak of World War II. The United States, which had dismantled its war propaganda apparatus in March 1919, felt in the late 1930s that the time had arrived to engage in some kind of limited cultural activity in Latin America. To that end, in May 1938, the State Department set up a section whose purpose was to expand hemispheric solidarity through fostering private scientific and cultural contacts.

While the Soviets used shortwave radio for clear political reasons and were followed in these techniques by Italy, Germany, and Japan, Western democracies began their shortwave radio programs to provide information to countrymen in their far-flung empires. The Netherlands started in 1927; the French followed in 1931; and Britain began in 1932. Each broadcast only in its national language. While other languages were added prior to World War II, they were generally translations of the original Dutch, French, or English language broadcasts.

During World War II, cultural propaganda was once again pushed into the background and political propaganda reigned supreme. Indeed, at the time of the outbreak of war only France still had a major unadulterated cultural propaganda effort. Political propaganda reached its pinnacle during the war with the creation of high-level departments in the United States and Britain to coordinate their psychological warfare activities. Propaganda was an important weapon in the belligerents' arsenal, supplementing military and economic arms. Unlike Germany, Italy, and the Soviet Union, which simply expanded their established propaganda departments, France, Britain, and the United States had to start almost from scratch. The British Ministry of Information was created only after the actual outbreak of war, and in the United States the Office of War Information was not founded until six months after America entered the war, though predecessor agencies had been in existence for several months and the Voice of America had started broadcasting within two months after Pearl Harbor.

At the end of the Second World War, as after the first, the various countries reverted to the *status quo ante bellum.* France resurrected its General Directorate for Cultural Affairs in the Quai d'Orsay. It gave new impetus to cultural communications and clearly separated it from political (or policy) information. In Germany, badly burned by Dr. Goebbels, cultural communications and policy information were also separated, with the former housed in the Foreign Office and the latter in the Chancellor's office. Britain, too, made a distinct separation between cultural communications (carried out by the semigovernmental British Council) and policy information, lodged in the Foreign Office. The Soviets, of course, continued in the same way as before; but even they made strenuous efforts to convince the outside world that cultural communications was separate from policy information. Only in the United States has the organizational distinction between policy information and cultural communications remained blurred.

In America, of course, there was no historical status quo to which to revert. Cultural communications had never existed independently of political propaganda. There was neither a national domestic radio service (like the BBC) which might absorb the Voice of America, nor a tradition of broadcasting overseas to one's own nationals. Cultural communications, policy information, and international radio broadcasting had all been born to fill the supreme political needs of war, and in the postwar era they were all turned to the equally urgent necessities of the Cold War. With the exception of academic exchanges, the same agency (the U.S. Information Agency) was given responsibility in 1953 for all three functions and directed to defend American foreign policy, portray American society abroad, and manage the Voice of America. USIA retains all those functions today.

Thus, historically, the American programs were almost as different from those of the other free-world governments as the latter had been from the totalitarian pattern of Nazi Germany and the Soviet Union. The program characteristics to which these differences have led in the postwar era are the subject of Chapter III.

III. THE PROGRAMS

The very importance of the United States in world politics today would seem to make it a target of prime importance for the policy information and cultural communications programs of other nations. A government wishing to impress with a particular foreign policy could do no better than to make an impression here, in the United States; success here means that an important part of the world is already persuaded, and (due to American leadership in the free world) that other conversions are likely on the way. But if the United States is the most influential society in the world, it is also among the most sophisticated. Americans will be difficult to persuade even if they can be reached with a particular message, and the highly developed American communications environment will make even the latter task extremely expensive and problematical. When the difficulties are added to the opportunities, it is doubtful whether any but the most wealthy nations could realistically elect to compete for the American mind.

It is these countries, the industrial elite of the late twentieth century, whose programs we have chosen to survey. The United States is one of them, for it conducts its own information and cultural programs in other industrial countries and finds there much the same kind of environment they face in the United States. As a group, these five nations are at or near the top in most standard indices of national power (arranged in Table 1). The GNP of the United States is about triple its nearest competitor, with Japan, Germany, France, and the United Kingdom following with rough

TABLE 1

	1973 GNP ($ Billions)	Territory (Million Sq. Miles)	Population (Millions)
U.S.	1,289	3.6	212
Japan	412	.14	110
F.R.G.	348	.1	62
France	239	.21	52
U.K.	175	.094	56

SOURCE: Cline, Ray S., **World Power Assessment,** Center for Strategic and International Studies, Georgetown University, 1975.

magnitudes from a third to a seventh as large. The United States also has the largest territorial domain and population. The other four countries have much smaller geographical areas, and all are far more densely populated than the United States.

As might be expected, the amounts spent by these countries on foreign affairs activities, including information and culture, vary considerably (see Table 2). In military spending, the United States, as leader of the free world, allocated over seven times as much as its nearest free world competitor in 1973. Yet in expenditures for information and culture the United States occupies a very different position. Here the leader of the free world ranks third in dollar amount and last in percentage of its annual budget spent on policy information and cultural communications. Both France, the leader in dollars spent, and Germany, a close second, rank ahead of the United States in their absolute level of resource commitment and far ahead in terms of the percentage of public funds earmarked for these

TABLE 2

1973 Data	Annual Budget $ Billion	Military Expenditures[⊕] $ Billion	% of Budget	Policy Information and Cultural Communications[§] $ Million	% of Budget
U.S.	276.7+	79.5	28.7	295+	.106
Britain	40.4	8.7	21.5	93	.230
F.R.G.	46.1	11.3	24.5	351	.761
France	46.7	8.4	18.0	487	1.042
Japan	54.5	3.5	6.4	80	.146

§ These figures include foreign aid related to information and cultural diplomacy.
+ **Budget of the U.S. Government, 1975.**
⊕ **The Military Balance, 1974-1975** (London: IISS, 1974).
SOURCES: **External Information and Cultural Relations Programs of Selected Countries,** 1973 (USIA)

programs. The smallest programs by far in dollar terms are those of Britain and Japan.

The amounts governments choose to spend on information and cultural programs are of course related to the motivations behind the programs and the objectives they try to serve. To examine these we must move country by country.[2]

France

Taken together, the French policy information and cultural communications programs are the biggest and best funded of any in the noncommunist world. Though with long historical antecedents, their importance among other foreign policy activities was greatly magnified after France's devasting experience in World War II, when these programs were seized upon as a surviving tool of French power that could contribute to reestablishing the country as a nation of the first rank. This perception expanded under de Gaulle's effort to carve out a distinctly independent political role as mediator between the two superpowers.

The basic organizational distinction between policy information and cultural communications is strictly maintained in France: press and information services that defend the government's short-term foreign policy interests are rigorously separated from the cultural program that is supposed to represent the enduring values and purposes incarnate in France, the nation. Thus, two directorates in the Ministry of Foreign Affairs are involved: the General Directorate for Cultural, Scientific, and Technical Relations handles cultural communications, while the Directorate of Information and Press Services deals with policy information within the General Directorate for Political Affairs.

Between the two programs, it is clearly cultural communications that receives the overwhelming emphasis. The Cultural Directorate General receives 50-60 percent of the Foreign Office's funds, whereas the Information and Press Directorate has only 6-7 percent. The heavy emphasis on cultural work and the broad public support it enjoys rest on two perceptions. First, there is the belief that France should do these things as the normal and expected activities of a great power, that there is a need to represent the French nation in the world and "bear witness" as an essential element in national identity. But second, the French believe that such activity will enhance French prestige and power and therefore inevitably facilitate accomplishment of the more specific and immediate purposes of French foreign policy. Both these ideas are rooted in the history of France as a nation particularly devoted to the arts and letters and convinced that French accomplishments in these aspects of civilization have given France a special world eminence and role—the famous *mission civilisatrice.*

The primary thematic emphasis of French cultural communications is the portrayal of France as a major nation with a stable and democratic government, a great moral and intellectual tradition, and a modern technologically and scientifically sophisticated economy. The policy information program, in addition to dealing with current political issues, draws upon the concept of France's civilizing mission as the foundation for two of its main themes. First, the policy information program points to the end of France's colonial empire and her high level of development aid (as well as her modest size) as evidence of affinity with smaller nations. Second, the spokesmen foster the idea of a need for French leadership and mediation in a world exposed to the dangers of superpower confrontation or—perhaps worse—condominium.

The relatively lower standing of France's policy information program is reflected in the allotment of personnel resources and a certain neglect of the media tools most appropriate for providing policy information. There are about 130 press counselors/attaches worldwide to execute the program, and they are supplied by teletype with the latest policy materials. Policy publications, photographic services, and TV and radio materials for local placement are also used. But international shortwave radio broadcasting is extremely low on the French list of media priorities. In the recent reorganization of the French radio system, overseas services emerged with only 99 broadcast hours per week, placing France last among our five countries in international broadcasts.

By contrast, the French emphasis on the older, slower cultural media is very strong, involving an enormous field network of cultural centers, institutes, and schools. Language instruction and book promotion are the two most important techniques for French cultural communications. The French teach more than a half-million language students abroad and manage to export 20 percent of their commercial book production. Official support for educational exchange is also vitally important in the French cultural effort: some 17,000 grantees come to France annually under French sponsorship, but the outward flow of 1,600 is almost entirely supported by other governments. The program is thus designed to expose others to France and not to send Frenchmen out to see the world. Film production is also of some importance as a cultural medium. Field outlets for French cultural communications include 145 cultural centers, 81 schools, and 1,200 centers of the semigovernmental Alliance Francaise, whose language teaching and other cultural activities supplement the official cultural program. There are over 300 center directors and librarians, 30,000 French teachers, and 104 embassy cultural counselors/attaches worldwide. It is a formidable cultural apparatus.

French cultural efforts are concentrated very heavily on Africa, in both the former French colonies on the Mediterranean and Francophone sub-Saharan Africa; together these take almost half of the program's resources. The next most important regions are Western Europe and Asia, each of which receives about 10 percent of the total effort. North America's share is an even smaller 5 percent. The reasons for this distribution are not far to seek—they relate to France's post-colonial attachments to Africa and to the deterioration of Franco-American relations in de Gaulle's regime.

The organization of French information and culture in Washington parallels the clear division between policy information and cultural communications found in the home organization. The two programs are handled by a press attache and a cultural counselor who coordinate their efforts informally but operate in a quite independent fashion. They are located, for example, in two different embassy buildings: the press attache at the embassy itself where he can be close to the ambassador, the cultural counselor at a separate site a half-hour's drive away. Similarly, they report to two different sets of people back home, one through the embassy political section to the Press and Information Directorate, the other directly to the Cultural Directorate General. Though the press attache is a career foreign service officer by profession, the cultural man is a teacher who as a member of the general French civil service can move from domestic to international education with ease. Physically, organizationally, and in staff background and training, the two services are thus quite distinct.

These distinctions are confirmed by a closer look at the major activities of these two programs in the United States. The press attache's work is highly political, concerned equally with explaining and defending policy positions of his government and reporting on the American press to authorities at home. His morning is spent preparing a five to eight page "Review of American Press" of the previous day, which goes out by teletype at noon to the Quai d'Orsay and certain embassies around the world. His afternoon is spent dealing with random questions about French foreign policy, preparing special dispatches to Paris on select subjects, and especially maintaining contacts with the Washington press corps. He is also responsibile for keeping the embassy staff informed of all U.S. press coverage in areas of their special interest and may see the ambassador as often as ten times a day on various public opinion issues.

To help him in these varied tasks the press attache has a Washington staff of six people, including himself. His principal assistant helps draft the morning press review and covers the Department of State, while another official covers the White House and Pentagon and maintains an office at the National Press Club. In gathering information from the press across the country the press attache is assisted by press officers in nine consulates at Boston, New York, Detroit, Chicago, San Francisco, Los Angeles, Honolulu, Houston, and New Orleans, each of whom has one or two assistants. Together they constitute the largest policy information field staff of any of the surveyed countries in the United States. These officials send reports concerning the press in their area to Washington each morning for inclusion in the daily review of the American press, and they also distribute information and documentation to sources in their local areas.

It is, in fact, only in this matter of information and documentation distribution that the French effort blurs the sharp distinction between policy information and culture. There is, in New York, a service of Information and Documentation with functions that belong essentially to cultural communications but which falls under the oversight of the Political Directorate. Its head is equal in rank to the Washington press attache and directs a staff of about 40 people. At one time the center of American press efforts by the French, today the service simply distributes set-piece documentation about France to those who request it: individuals, associations, researchers, university personnel, students, and others. The service also publishes a weekly press bulletin, covering such items as speeches of French officials and other news of France, to be sent to 28,000 public opinion leaders in the United States.

Why do the French operate so extensive a policy information program here, and what do they hope to accomplish? The French program is based on the explicit realization that the press is vital to the opinion-making process in the United States, and that it is therefore necessary to maintain contact with its representatives in order to further acceptance of French foreign policy. In carrying out these responsibilities embassy officials feel that they are materially aided by the lack of a sense of hierarchy on the part of the U.S. press corps, which makes it possible to see key people with relative ease. They are hindered by what they consider to be strongly anti-French public opinion here which sees France as a nation ungrateful for U.S. aid after World War II and points to its conduct toward the United States and NATO during the Gaullist era as proof. Those running France's policy information program hope to persuade Americans that it is wrong to resent France's independent position and that there is long-range value for the United States to have an ally that possesses the means and the will for independent action but that agrees fundamentally on the values of democracy and Western civilization. In this, indeed, the French press service comes closest to a central objective: convincing the American people that, though difficult to manage in the short run, an ally such as France provides a great element of strength to the Western alliance.

As far as French cultural efforts are concerned, there seems to be a much less defined sense of objective and theme. The self-justifying nature of the program in Paris, where cultural dissemination is seen as one of those activities in which a great nation engages, is amply reflected in French cultural operations in the United States. French cultural diplomatists hope to persuade Americans that Paris is not simply a cultural province of New York and that even in the postwar era Paris stands on its own as a major cultural center with a great deal that is uniquely French to offer the world. This, the French say, is a very difficult task, for Americans are felt to be poorly informed about France and tend to see it as the nation of wine, perfume, and high fashion. Still there is apparently no conscious effort to put forward a specific aspect of France to counteract this image, or to design a program around specific objectives and themes. Nor is the program targeted to specific opinion leaders in the United States. Virtually no evaluative effort is made because the program is seen as qualitative, not quantitative. Indeed, even to ask how a governmental program can exist without clear operational objectives was considered a strangely "American" question!

The French cultural program in the United States is therefore rigidly divorced from all political objectives. As if to emphasize that fact, the main part of the program is located in New York City, far away from the political pressures of the national capital.[3] At present there are some 50 people in New York, but a staff of only six in Washington. There are also cultural attaches at four French Consulates (New York, San Francisco, Los Angeles, and New Orleans) and combined cultural-scientific officers at two others (Houston and Boston). In spite of the much larger budget of the overall cultural program in the French effort, its U.S. staff is thus really about the same size as that of the press section, perhaps a reflection of the fact that the United States is considered the most important country for the worldwide policy information effort but ranks down the list of geographic priorities for the cultural side.

Bereft as they are of specific cultural objectives, the New York and Washington offices spend their time in the administration of routine cultural activities in the United States. The New York office writes and publishes pamphlets about French culture that are distributed to correspondents and sent for distribution to cultural attaches. It has an audiovisual department that ships French films all over the United States and arranges for placement of TV programs, an art section that schedules cultural presentations in the United States, and a department that handles small travelling exhibitions. New York also spends a good deal of time on the exchange of persons program, arranging short-term visits (two weeks to three months) of researchers, professors, film directors, and politicos—35 to 40 per year in each direction.

The Washington office operates both as a national adjunct to the New York operation and as a local consulate-type service for the Washington, D.C. area. In its national role it runs the French scholarship and assistantship program and oversees French schools in the United States. The scholarship program is responsible for 250 French graduate students in the United States (mostly studying business administration, architecture, and medicine), and about 100 American Ph.D. candidates in France (concentrated in French language and the sciences). The assistantship program is responsible for the exchange of 50 to 60 graduate students each way each year, to work in universities as French or English resource people. Finally, the Washington office supervises the five French schools in the United States, but puts little money into them beyond that of the director's salary and an occasional French teacher.

The local work of the Washington office is roughly the same as that of consulates across the country. Most important is the dissemination of materials (from books and teaching materials to films) about the French language and French culture to educational institutions and other interested groups in the metropolitan area. Efforts to promote the French language—always vitally important in the French program—are also made through support of the local association of French teachers at schools and nearby universities. A very important activity is the publication of a local bulletin of dates and places of French-language activities in the area each month, sent to members of the cultural community. Cultural presentations and exhibits in the region are also the responsibility of the local consulate, as is attention to visitors on the exchange program.

Finally, French cultural efforts are assisted by some 230 American chapters of the Alliance Francaise, coordinated by a federation in New York. Half a dozen or more of these are large chapters with their own buildings, libraries, cultural events, and so forth, some with memberships as high as 900 and heavily involved in language teaching. Most are small university groups of 15-20 members. None receive funds from the French government, but all are supported by gifts of instructural materials and library books from the French cultural program.

Federal Republic of Germany

Like the modern French program, information and cultural efforts of the Federal Republic also developed in their present form out of the traumatic experience of World War II. Here of course the need was not so much the reestablishment of a great nation but the rehabilitation of its international reputation after the ravages of Nazism. The task was to be accomplished through emphasis on values in the German tradition anti-thetical to Nazism: humanism, internationalism, pluralism, and the traditional German arts and letters—in a word, *Kultur.* Since the mid-1960s, with the period of German expiation ended, *Kulturpolitik* has been brought to the service of new goals and given equal status with political and economic diplomacy as a "third pillar" of German foreign policy.

Organizationally, the German arrangement, though differing from the French in its extreme decentralization, follows a similar separation of the political from the cultural. The Federal Press and Information Office functions directly under the Chancellor's office and is headed by his appointee, whereas the Department for External Cultural Policy is a part of the Foreign Office. Even for budgetary purposes the two programs are considered quite independent of each other.

Judging by program size, cultural communication is more important to Germany than policy information, though the imbalance is not so extreme as in the French case. In recent years the budget of the Foreign Ministry's Department of External Cultural Policy has been increased while that of the Federal Press and Information Office has been gradually eroded by inflation, so that today the former is more than five times the size of the latter.

The policy information program is carried out by 56 full-time and 23 part-time press attaches in German embassies abroad. Its themes revolve around the central idea that Germany desires international cooperation and peaceful relations with all nations. Specifically, this means partnership with other Western democracies, multilateralism within the European Economic Community, and peaceful coexistence with communist countries, especially East Germany. In support of those themes the International Division of the Federal Press and Information Office concentrates its media resources in periodicals and newspapers, film and TV production, and foreign visitors, in that order, with books, pamphlets, and teletyped materials receiving less emphasis. International shortwave radio broadcasting, however, is a very important medium for Germany. *Deutsche Welle* and *Deutschlandfunk,* the worldwide and European services, together broadcast 768 hours per week, making Germany second in this activity among the five countries surveyed.

West German cultural communications in its early years was focused on German achievement in the arts and letters and concentrated on a narrow and generally Germanophile cultural elite in foreign countries, particularly Latin America. Today the program is more concerned with portraying the whole spectrum of German life, appealing to a broader foreign audience of "multipliers" who in turn can transmit the message to the masses. Themes now are the economic, scientific, and technological achievements of the Federal Republic, the stability of its institutions, and mobility in the West German social structure. There is a new concern for credibility and faithfulness to the reality of German life. A major effort is underway to make the program more reciprocal by using local talent overseas and balancing the exchange program with more German students abroad on government aid. Finally, there has been a geographical shift in emphasis away from Latin America and toward Eastern and Western Europe and, to some extent, the United States.

The two primary vehicles of German cultural communications are still the German language and German schools abroad. Although Germany has only a handful of teachers serving overseas (less than 2,000) compared to France, it devotes more than a quarter of the Cultural Department's budget to the support of 250 German schools. The Federal Republic also has a large and expanding exchange program in academic, youth, and vocational areas run by a variety of foundations that are in turn often supported by government funds. Most prominent among these is the German Academic Exchange Service (DAAD), which handles the academic program. It is just one of 10 or more so-called intermediary organizations that help execute the extremely decentralized German cultural communications program. Most important overseas are the 114 branches of the Goethe Institute— a semigovernmental organization supported by government funds that actually programs the bulk of Germany's cultural activities abroad.

The most obvious fact about the German information and cultural program in the United States is that it places far more emphasis on cultural communications than on policy information. Those running both programs insist, to be sure, that the United States is their most important country, but the emphasis on culture is in line with the worldwide priority Germany gives to cultural communications over policy information. In personnel allocation alone the cultural section of the Washington embassy can boast of a 10-man staff whereas the press office has only six, a manpower distribution the reverse of that in the French embassy. In addition, the cultural program operates four branches of the Goethe Institute across the country at Boston, New York, Atlanta, and San Francisco, with a fifth planned for Chicago, the largest such network of any of the countries surveyed. Perhaps as a result of the resources absorbed by the Goethe Institutes, the German program has a smaller staff outside the capital than does France: only two cultural officers (New York and Chicago) as compared to six for the French, and four press officers (Boston, New York, Chicago, and Los Angeles) as compared to nine. Yet there is no question that for the Germans culture is the dominant concern.

A closer look at the two programs confirms this impression of priorities. The activities of the press and information section in the Washington embassy seem to be roughly similar to those of the French press office, though rather less time is spent cultivating contacts with the local media. Answering a steady stream of questions and inquiries about Germany takes up a good deal of the section's time, as does preparing for the visits of prominent German officials to the United States and taking care of them while here. In addition, considerable effort is devoted simply to keeping up with the news in the United States by monitoring the wire services and the press with the help of the consulate press officers. In this regard the embassy depends upon the press section to be its eyes and ears in the United States and keep it informed of local developments. No daily digest of the American press is sent to Bonn, though an average of two cables a day are dispatched on bilaterial topics of current press interest. In addition the section keeps in close contact with about 30 foreign correspondents of German newspapers here, both to collect information they gather in press conferences and to help them improve their coverage of American affairs back home. Finally, the press and information office runs a piece of the exchange of visitors program, sending about 50 newspaper people to Germany each year for a two-week visit and receiving lecturers who deal with political topics here in the United States.

The press section is greatly assisted by the German Information Center in New York, an organization of 25 to 30 people who (as in the French system) handle the production and distribution of routine material in the United States.[4] They distribute films and booklets on Germany, deal with TV and radio personnel in the city, and publish specialized papers including a daily "Relay from Bonn" on political events plus occasional economic and social reports. Most of this material does not advocate German foreign policy and therefore really serves the cultural communications function.

The German press section also spends considerable effort in evaluating the effectiveness of the different media. Personal contact, the exchange of visitors and lecturers, and films are rated most effective, followed by the distribution of periodicals and exhibitions. Still lower on the scale are TV spots and the placement of articles and pictures in the American press—

media which are virtually impossible to use in the saturated American communications environment. Clearly the press effort here is a highly targeted one, primarily concerned with cultivating influential people.

Before turning to German cultural communications, it is important to point out that the separation between it and the policy information side in Washington is as distinctly maintained as in the French system. The political character of the press office is clearly recognized but, remembering Nazi politicization of culture, every effort is made to protect the cultural arm from contamination. Though he exchanges information with the cultural counselor by phone on a daily basis, the press counselor carries out his duties quite separately from his cultural opposite number. The two men report back to different sections of the Foreign Office: the press counselor to the Information Desk which in turn is linked to the international division in the Chancellor's Federal Press and Information Office, the cultural counselor to the Department for External Cultural Policy. They do share to a certain extent the German Information Service in New York (though it falls organizationally under the policy information area), but political exchanges are kept separate from cultural exchanges.

Perhaps most important in the separation of the two and the protection of German cultural programs from political influence is the fact that the cultural program is mainly carried out by four branches of the Goethe Institute. They maintain libraries, teach the latest techniques of German language instruction, arrange concerts and lectures, and set up films and exhibits. Efforts are not directed chiefly at establishing the institutes as the locale for German-American contact; rather, they emphasize leaving the premises to seek out American partners and set up activities with American counterparts. Thematically, the institutes place emphasis on modern Germany, her sociology, educational system, economic development, and so forth, subjects which are treated objectively and without advocacy of the German policy line.

The breadth of work undertaken by the Goethe Institutes reduces the cultural counselor and his staff to a role that is essentially advisory and supplementary. Educational exchange arrangements occupy a considerable amount of their time, since the Fulbright program and the German Academic Exchange Association are responsible for some 200 Americans going to the Federal Republic annually. The majority of these are students of German language and literature, though the embassy is trying to extend the selection process to less academic categories, such as trade unionists, journalists, and congressional aides. Although the cultural counselor does give advice on the directions these programs ought to assume, the actual selection of candidates is always given to outside organizations in order to avoid the political problems associated with the embassy handing out scholarships. The cultural counselor rates such activities his number one priority, on the theory that people who spend time in Germany will "get to know us better" and be disabused of misconceptions about the German people.

The second media priority for the German cultural program in the United States is probably language instruction, given in the Goethe Institutes not to "end consumers" but to teachers. Here the cultural staff at the embassy helps by supporting associations of teachers of German, offering periodicals, study materials, seminars, and youth clubs. The embassy staff also plays an important support role for the German School in Washington, attended by 650 students (of whom 40 percent are non-German). Cultural presentations are often scheduled by the New York consulate officer via Goethe Institutes, but though expensive they are not of relatively great importance to the German effort here. Of still lower priority is the scheduling of small exhibits, and the distribution through the consulates and by the German Information Center in New York of brochures, pamphlets, books, and films.

What, then, are the goals of this information and cultural effort? Here the Germans seem to have thought through their objectives more carefully than have the French, possibly because of their closer political relationship to the United States. Though smaller than that devoted to all of Western Europe, this is the biggest single-country program in the German program worldwide, and it is so because of the need felt by Germany to underscore the existing alliance. As the smaller partner in that alliance the Federal Republic feels it needs to make the United States take notice of it; to put it differently, the Germans intend to show that they are America's most important ally and that the United States would not be as well off without Germany. This means, for the cultural program, presenting Germany as a country that can be proud of its culture both past and present—a country worth being interested in. It involves presenting a credible picture, the bad with the good, and establishing partnerships with Americans that look to the recognition and solution of common problems as well as the demonstration of mutual interests. For the policy information program it means dealing with the public opinion problem of the moment—be it fears of *Ostpolitik* going too far, worries about an economic crisis leading to a resurgence of Nazi sentiment, or the perception that German economic strength makes possible a reduction of American support for her German ally.

In all these efforts the Germans, in marked contrast to the French, believe that they are working against a background of success. They are convinced that postwar prejudice has just about disappeared, helped by the exchange of soldiers and tourists and a marked improvement in reporting about Germany. Now the embassy sees its task as simply to deepen and enlarge the atmosphere of mutual understanding and friendship that already exists.

United Kingdom

British information and cultural programs have been less influenced by the trauma of World War II than those of France or Germany. They are the product, instead, of the combination of much older traditions with the difficult position Britain has faced since the war's end. Among these older traditions are a strong belief in freedom of information as a first political principle, coupled with insistence on objectivity and reliability. Simultaneously, the paradoxical aftermath of British victory in the war has required adaptation to an era of national decline along with support for a continuing British role in the postwar world.

Organizationally, the British model is more complicated than the French and German ones but maintains the separation of policy information from cultural comunications. Generally speaking, cultural relations are in the hands of the semigovernmental British Council, while policy information is handled in the Foreign and Commonwealth Office.

Four general foreign policy objectives are currently supported by British policy information and cultural communications:

(1) A recent development is export promotion to increase the sale of British goods overseas and to help reverse Britain's chronic postwar trade deficit. Two-thirds of the output of the Central Office of Information (COI), the major media production outfit in the British system, deals with commercial promotion.

(2) A second objective is closely related to Britain's need to trade: therefore, a goal is the achievement of a stable and peaceful world, where trade will be uninterrupted

(3) Britain uses her information and cultural programs to foster strong and friendly relationships with various nations and major groups of nations, such as NATO, the Organization for Economic Co-operation and Development, the Common Market states, and of course the British Commonwealth.

(4) Finally, the British share the general goal of preventing the spread of Soviet communism.

Functioning under these objectives, British policy information worldwide covers both political and economic themes. On the political side,

British information and press officers try to show that Britain is a trustworthy and stalwart ally, that in spite of economic difficulties she has the economic and military power and the will to oppose aggression and contribute to Third World development. Among the less-developed countries, the British argue that the democratic model provides a more attractive and successful road to economic and social progress than communism. Commercially, the effort is to show that Britain is a desirable trading partner who must trade to live and therefore will be both a good customer and a good merchant.

Themes in British cultural communications reinforce these arguments by portraying relevant aspects of British society. The United Kingdom is represented as a highly civilized and stable society that has given the world parliamentary government, the Anglo-Saxon legal system with its great emphasis on individual liberty, the near-universal English language, and a respectable liquidation of her vast colonial empire. Commercial objectives are supported by a portrayal of British economic life showing British workmen to be highly skilled craftsmen, working in a tradition of high quality yet backed by the latest scientific and technological capabilities. And finally there is the living example of freedom of information at work, as a vital element in Britain's internal life and as reflected in her efforts to provide to denied areas information of all sorts that is withheld by their governments.

The content of British programs outlined by these thematic emphases is given life through their unique style. Most important, perhaps, is the British flair for understatement and a certain detached reserve. British programs are pitched at rather a high intellectual level, and there is a definite effort in that way to select or target the influential few in foreign countries. On the cultural side, generalization is avoided, the aim being to generate an overall picture of British society in the mind of the audience as the cumulative effect of many small portrayals of selected specific aspects of British life.

British policy information programs are executed overseas by information counselors or attaches who in the larger countries supervise what are called the British Information Services (BIS). They pass out large quantities of feature material on British subjects produced under the Foreign Office's direction by the Central Office of Information. Some of this is policy information, but most is cultural in nature and deals with the British economy, government, royal family, tourism, and so forth. In addition, commercial exhibits are an important part of the policy information effort.

The BBC external services now broadcast 761 hours per week, third among our five countries. While often thought of as a policy information medium, the BBC is a cultural and news medium too, set up so as to be insulated from political pressures. It carries the foreign policy line of the government as one story among many.

British cultural communications overseas are in the hands of the British Council, a quasi-governmental organization like the Alliance Française and the Goethe Institute, functioning outside the Foreign Office under an independent board but financed by governmental funds. Activities of the British Council, and especially the exchange of persons, have increased in recent years. Its major activity is English teaching, which is seen as an essential fulcrum for all the other British Council work. The council also operates libraries and book distribution, where the recent emphasis is on making the library a contact point between the foreign professional and sources of information in the United Kingdom. The growing exchange of persons is a third focus of activity; the Council handles technical and academic exchanges, with 36 percent of its budget used to bring nearly 21,000 exchangees to the United Kingdom yearly. The council is also the focal point for cultural presentations and art exhibits, although these are less and less used. The council now has 115 centers in 82 countries and about 120 libraries, four out of five located in the developing world.

Geographically, the British information and cultural programs center on two kinds of areas. First in priority are the advanced industrial countries most closely associated politically and commercially with Britain, such as Western Europe, the United States, and Japan. Secondly, though perhaps first in distribution of resources, are the Commonwealth nations, followed by the rest of the Third World.

A striking characteristic of the British effort in the United States is its almost exclusive emphasis on policy information over cultural communications, exactly opposite to the German program. The information counselor and his staff at the embassy in Washington number 16, by far the biggest of the countries surveyed, whereas there are only two cultural attaches, the smallest such contingent. The reason for this distribution of resources is said to be the preexistent cultural affinity between the two countries—the common heritage, especially of language and democratic parliamentary traditions. The presence of these factors allows for so great a volume of natural cultural exchange across the Atlantic that there is felt to be little need or room for a governmental program. Indeed, until very recently there was not even a cultural attache in Washington!

The British do, of course, maintain in New York the usual bulk-mailing service for routine distribution of information about all facets of British life and politics. It is called the British Information Service, and its 70-odd people are equally divided between distribution of commercial and cultural information. They produce reviews of the British press and statements of ministers for distribution to newspapers and the general public, as well as a wide range of film and written production aimed at the inquiring public and trade journals.

The large policy information staff in Washington, backed by the New York BIS and by full-time information officers in three of the 11 British consulates (Boston, Los Angeles, and San Francisco), manifests very clear political and commercial *raisons d'être*. Its basic objective is to "keep the United Kingdom visible"—favorably visible—in the United States, and this is done for a series of perfectly specific reasons. On the political side, visibility is needed to convince the American people that Britain is a reliable partner whose views should be taken into account in the formation of policy. British policy information thus can be viewed as a tool for the recovery, through influence on the United States, of some of the power in world affairs that Britain has lost in recent years. On the economic side the United States is vitally important as Britain's biggest market and investor; here the British want Americans to see the United Kingdom as a country they would like to visit and buy from. This commercial thrust is estimated to account for about half of Britain's information and cultural effort in the United States.

The techniques used by the information counselor and his staff for keeping Britain visible seem in large part responsive and tend to revolve (as in most information programs) around issues rather than themes. Some 20,000 calls from the general public are answered each year by the Washington staff, but the British information program tries to be a highly targeted one that interests itself primarily in "multipliers," particularly in the mass media. Hence, possibly the most important part of the information officer's job is to establish and keep open a network of media contacts that are available for use when needed, while at the same time keeping informed in order to be able to use those contacts effectively. Recent issues in this effort range from the Concorde to the economic situation in Britain to the influence of American financial contributions on the turmoil in Ireland.

In its desire to keep Britain visible the embassy's information section (like its German equivalent) also runs a small and highly-targeted exchange of persons program, through which about a dozen prominent opinion leaders move each way annually. Of those coming to the United States (programmed out of New York), about half are political figures and half are leading academics specializing generally in recent history and political science. Those invited to Britain are likely to be governors, mayors, congressional aides, editors—and some key businessmen. In addition, the embassy staff often holds predeparture briefings for professional people going to England and then facilitates their contact with leading Britons once arrived.

Finally, the embassy's information section appears to perform the opinion and press monitoring and advisory functions rather less elaborately than other embassies we have examined. It does have a press cutting section, fed by the consulates, which sees to it that relevant embassy staff are kept informed of American developments in their areas of interest. But there is no daily review of the American press sent back home on the French model; each section of the embassy reports back on its own activities and occasionally the press section will supplement their work with an overall piece on the "mood" of the American public. The information counselor, a foreign service officer, does see the ambassador daily and acts as his public relations advisor and publicity agent. He considers these functions a most important part of his job.

Viewed in the perspective of this large and active policy information effort, the British cultural program in the United States appears slender. Its two officers are members of the British Council staff, assigned to the embassy as education attaches. There are no British Council offices here in the United States—in striking contrast to the German Goethe Institutes. There are also no cultural officers in the consulates, though the consul general himself or his information officer may help if needed. This lack of staff means that many of the functions normally performed by a cultural program are not found in the British effort here. There are no British schools here, cultural presentations are not governmentally funded, and there is of course no English language teaching. It also means that much of what the embassy does is in the nature of "plugging into" American activities, using a very sparse budget as seed money and to show token support. Thus performing artists already here are given receptions and assistance with facilities; art exhibitions may be programmed or a catalogue printed at embassy expense; and great amounts of time are absorbed simply in maintaining liaison with American governmental and private institutions (Smithsonian, Carnegie, Ford) active in cultural matters.

The rest and largest part of the British cultural effort here is devoted to education. Indirectly, the cultural program supports education through liaison with American educators, exchanging ideas on the latest British and American methods. The educational attache spends a considerable part of his time travelling throughout the United States, finding out what universities are doing. Directly, the program supports education through a modest exchange of persons program, including exchange of about 100 secondary school teachers annually and the administration of the prestigious Marshall Scholarship program that selects some 25 outstanding American university graduates for study in Britain annually. The cultural staff also serves the ambassador as his advisor on matters of education and culture.

Japan

Any analysis of the information and cultural programs of Japan must begin with the fact that, though growing, they are the smallest of the countries we are surveying. In part this is a reflection of Japan's overall role in the world; stunted by her wartime record, Japan the industrial giant has only recently and still with reluctance begun to play a major political role on the world stage. In addition, however, the Japanese have an innate sense of the uniqueness of their culture and society. In striking contrast to the French, it is not in their national character to spread their culture about the world. Furthermore, Japan labors under extreme limitations because of the sharpness of cultural differences and because her difficult language generally precludes direct foreign access to things Japanese except in the visual arts and music. As a result Japan is a net importer of culture from the world, greatly influenced by foreign TV, books, and thought, but influencing them little. The flow of both people and media is inward, making Japan the most "reciprocal" of nations.

Because of their common insular positions, the foreign policy objectives that Japan's information and cultural programs are designed to serve bear some superficial relationship to those of the United Kingdom. As a trading nation, Japan is interested primarily in ensuring her economic security; that is, safeguarding her ability to purchase raw materials abroad and sell manufactures there to pay for those imports. In contrast to Britain's situation, however, Japan's great success in export trade has produced an emphasis on making success palatable abroad rather than trying to overcome difficulties. Like the United Kingdom, Japan depends upon a peaceful and stable world order in which to carry on trade, and this is a key Japanese objective. Additionally, Japanese programs devote attention to the development of bilateral relationships with key trading and security partners (especially the United States and Southeast Asia).

Organizationally, the situation in Japan is not quite as clear-cut as in France, Germany, and Britain. Until very recently, there was only a single Bureau of Public Information and Cultural Affairs in the Foreign Office, which handled both information and culture. Today the program is conducted by two directorates, a Public Information and Press Directorate and a Cultural Exchange Directorate. There is, moreover, the recently formed quasi-private Japan Foundation to carry out cultural work abroad outside the embassy. Yet official information and cultural work is still administered overseas by a single embassy officer, and the older pattern of unity has apparently not yet been significantly altered.

Thematically, the Japanese policy information program focuses on a variety of economic and security issues. Japan's economic themes concentrate on dispelling so-called myths about Japan's competitive success—such as that Japan's prosperity is based on cheap Oriental labor, or that the Japanese government subsidizes export industries and shuts out foreign products through high tariff and nontariff trade barriers. Japanese programs emphasize that although Japan is dependent upon trade, she does not take unfair or discriminatory advantage of competitors and maintains an economy as open as that of any major industrialized country. Politically, Japan points to her pacific foreign policy since World War II and her proud acceptance of a constitution that forbids recourse to war as an instrument of national policy. She argues for support of the United Nations (with a Security Council strengthened by permanent Japanese representation) and arms control. Japan publicly declares that developed countries should support the growth needs of the Third World up to 1 percent of their GNPs, thus indicating her support for the aspirations of her Asian trading partners. Finally, she asserts that the U.S.-Japanese alliance is indispensable not only for both countries but also for the peace of the world.

Japanese cultural communications, by contrast, seem to have little thematic direction. The style of the program is extremely low-key, to the point that most cultural materials simply deal with Japanese life and people without any apparent thematic purpose except to inform people overseas about this highly unfamiliar country. Insofar as there is a conscious thematic content, Japan tries to portray a society with deep traditions worthy of respect but infused with an eclectic acceptance of modern, Western values—a free society with democratic institutions and all the problems of any highly industrialized nation. The general idea is to prove that, though culturally different, the Japanese remain reliable and comprehensible people with whom international intercourse is possible and pleasant.

The fast media, so important to policy information programs, are rather of low priority for Japan. Radio Japan, the overseas service of NHK, is a declining stock in the Japanese communications portfolio—its budget has been held stationary for a number of years. Perhaps this is because it is used principally as a policy information medium, with two-thirds of its programming devoted to news and commentary. NHK broadcasts 259 hours per week in 21 languages, fourth among the five countries surveyed here. The Japanese believe that shortwave reaches only radio buffs and is therefore an inefficient medium. Television placement overseas is extremely difficult for the Japanese, again because of the language problem, though domestic Japanese television is heavily influenced by foreign products—another example of Japan's cultural import surplus. Recognizing that most news of Japan overseas is generated by outside agencies, the Japanese are deeply concerned with facilitative assistance to foreign news professionals. Almost 500 foreign journalists are aided by the Foreign Ministry yearly, and some 50 two-week tours of Japan are given to foreign journalists each year.

Japanese cultural communications rely on the slower media common to most cultural programs. But language and other cultural barriers make several techniques used by other countries of little importance for Japan. The concept of an information center with a library at its heart plays no role in the Japanese program, for example. There are only 26 information centers around the world, most of them in the nonpriority areas of Europe and Latin America, and they act mostly as distribution posts for such material as is available in the local language. Libraries do not exist for lack of books in translation, and the difficult Japanese language is taught only sporadically. Centers do provide a forum for occasional cultural presentations and some exhibits, but their role is extremely modest. Films are somewhat more important, particularly in developing areas where the emphasis is on a mass audience and the content is strictly cultural. Prestige publications are also an important part of the Japanese program, where it is felt that elaborate printing techniques do something for one's technological image.

The media mainstay of the Japanese program is exchange of persons, handled by a new organization, the Japan Foundation. Liberally funded by a government endowment of over $100 million, the foundation was established outside the Foreign Office in order to separate cultural communications from policy information. It seems to be mainly a headquarters operation and devotes most of its annual operating budget of over $8 million to exchange activites. Exchanges, the best-funded single activity in the Japanese program, doubled between 1971 and 1974, when over 12,000 government-sponsored exchanges took place, with two-thirds of these outbound from Japan and roughly 40 percent for educational purposes. The Japan Foundation has placed its emphasis on professional exchanges and direct grants to foreign universities to establish Japanese studies programs overseas.

Though theirs is still a small program, the Japanese have a clear sense of where it is going, and this extends to target areas. Here the United

States is designated unambiguously as "irreplaceably important" to Japan and the number one priority. Next comes East and Southeast Asia, the greatest source of raw materials for Japan and collectively the greatest purchaser of Japanese goods. Third is Western Europe, due to its industrial status and to free world ties and political similarities. At lower levels of importance are the Middle East (the oil connection), the Soviet Union, the People's Republic of China, Australia, and New Zealand.

Of all the countries surveyed in this study, Japan concentrates the greatest proportion of its worldwide information and cultural program on the United States. In budgetary terms almost a third of the Foreign Ministry's program goes to the United States, and half the Japan Foundation's funds are committed here. Partially this allocation reflects the intrinsic importance of the United States in Japan's overall foreign policy, since it is both the principal guarantor of Japanese security and her largest trading partner. But the allocation is also based on the belief that information and cultural efforts here have acceleration or multiplier effects worldwide, that the U.S. role in the international flow of information is so important that achieving an understanding of Japan here will materially affect the achievement of a similar understanding elsewhere.

The high priority given to the United States by Japan does not, however, mean that the Japanese effort here is larger than that of its industrialized competitors. The Japanese program is probably somewhere in between the French or German programs and the British effort in size. There are five Japanese information/cultural officers in the Washington embassy assisted by eight Americans. There are small information centers in New York and San Francisco staffed by 10 people or fewer, but only one information/cultural officer among Japan's 12 consulates. Finally, the Japan Foundation maintains two U.S. offices, in Washington and New York, each staffed by four or five people. Though large by Japanese standards, it is in competitive terms a modest program.

Organizationally, the Japanese program in the United States is unique as the only unified program among the major industrialized countries. There is no organizational differentiation within the embassy between policy information and cultural communications, with both under the direction of a single so-called "information" counselor. This may be partially explained as an inheritance from an era when Japanese programs were much smaller and staffing was insufficient for a divided program, but the Japanese explain that information and culture aim at the same thing—to inform people about Japan—and therefore should be administered as one. In practice, the result is that the information counselor and his deputy handle press relations, while the three other officers take care of cultural promotion, academic liason, and education. The division of emphasis between information and culture appears to be roughly equal.

Functionally, the Japanese information program seems quite similar to its Western counterparts. The information counselor and his deputy spend their time in personal contact with American and Japanese journalists, keeping them up to date and accurate on Japanese life and policy; Americans on their staffs devote their efforts to answering telephone and written inquiries; the information centers in New York and San Francisco turn out the standard kinds of pamphlets and materials on Japanese life and thought to satisfy the curious in the United States; the embassy collates press clippings from the consulates into a daily report on American public opinion for Tokyo. The cultural effort is unusual, however, in that there are no cultural centers, no language instruction, no libraries, few exhibits, and only one small school. Instead, the Japanese concentrate on exchange of persons, aid to American universities, and cultural promotion, with all three functions divided between the Japan Foundation and the embassy.

The foundation's efforts in the United States are differentiated from the embassy's cultural program in being highly specialized and aiming at the postgraduate level, whereas the embassy's cultural work is aimed at young people generally. The foundation thus runs lecture series, gives aid and instructional materials to universities, subsidizes American appearances by Japanese performing artists, and runs the scholarship program. One million dollars has been given to each of 10 American universities to support departments of Japanese studies, making the program perhaps the most heavily targeted at the university level of any we have surveyed. The exchange-of-persons program backs up this emphasis, annually sending from 300 to 500 Japanese to the United States and about 100 Americans to Japan.

Two themes run through Japanese information and cultural efforts in the United States. The first holds that there is an essential ground of common humanity between the American and Japanese people on which they can meet despite wide cultural differences. The Japanese, in other words, are not inscrutable Orientals but understandable people, many of whose differences from Westerners result naturally from the different circumstances of their lives. This is not to say that Japanese try to minimize the cultural differences that exist between East and West; indeed, the cultural events they schedule indicate some desire to emphasize the unique and exotic about Japanese life as an attraction for Western audiences. But there is some ambivalence here in Japanese programming, for at the same time they worry about projecting stereotyped images of Japan through lectures on flower arranging and performances of Kabuki dancers.

In spite of this apparent contradiction, the second theme makes the corollary point that American and Japanese societies are alike in many fundamental respects, particularly in their common devotion to parliamentary democracy and their need to face and solve the many problems of postindustrial life. The Japanese then point out that the existence of areas of political, economic, and social similarity provides many opportunities for fruitful interchange between the United States and Japan: for example, environmental protection, law and order, and labor-management relations. They hope to bring together people who can cooperate in these areas.

The major theme in the Japanese policy information program in the United States explains and defends Japan's special role in the postwar world. Japanese officials believe that many Americans interpret Japan's extremely cautious foreign policy as a shirking of its international political duty, in view of its economic power. In response, Japanese diplomats stress that Japan must be cautious because of her great economic and small military power. She must not give small countries in her area the feeling that she is trying to "corner" them, and at the same time she must maintain open channels of trade to supply the home islands. Moreover, they suggests that the cautious and pacific tenor of Japanese foreign policy might well commend itself to other powers as a model that, if widely followed, would contribute substantially to world peace.

Japanese officials know that their information and cultural program in the United States is fraught with difficulty. Americans' attention in international affairs generally, they feel, is directed toward Europe, the Soviet Union, and the Middle East. Japan must compete with these preoccupations. The difficulties are enhanced by cultural differences, which make it hard for Japanese diplomatists to reach confident conclusions about American opinion and ideas. Public relations firms and consultants are used (absorbing up to about 10 percent of the budget) to overcome this lack of empathy, but they create the danger that the cultural effort will be dominated by outsiders. Japan attempts to overcome this in turn by large doses of personal contact, an expensive task. It is a difficulty for which there is no easy solution.

It has been recently revealed (Washington Post, 1976) that the Japanese government also provides 90 percent of the funding behind the United States-Japan Trade Council, a Washington-based outfit run by American citizens since 1957. It carries on extensive policy information work with influential American columnists and journalists, both in the broadcast and print media, in order to offset the negative impact of the U.S. trade deficit with Japan. The council sends journalists and congressional aides to Japan, holds conferences of high level academic and government leaders to present Japanese viewpoints, distributes films to American schools, and has lobbied extensively in Congress for measures favorable to Japanese trade and against legislation that would hurt it. The council has not until recently admitted that the Japanese government provides its financial support and as a result is faced with civil fraud charges by the American Department of Justice.

United States

The U.S. information and cultural programs are conducted by the United States Information Agency, a governmental organization whose director reports to the president, and by the State Department's Bureau of Educational and Cultural Affairs, which is responsible for one segment of the cultural program: the exchange of persons. Cultural communications are thus split between two agencies according to media functions: the Educational and Cultural Affairs Bureau (CU) handles people, whereas the independent USIA handles "things"—that is, all other media. Policy information is also split between State Department political officers and USIA personnel, since the latter are supposed (in addition to their cultural duties) to explain and defend United States government policy overseas. In a sense, then, information and culture are both combined and divided in the American model: combined in USIA, but divided between it and other organizations (State/CU for cultural communications and State/Political for policy information). The organizational division does not follow the functional lines pursued by other Western governments.

Almost every diplomatic mission has a USIA officer, who may in small posts double as a policy information and cultural communications officer. Some posts have only one American officer while others have as many as 38 (Brazil). At this writing, there are 188 posts in 122 countries. The total budget for USIA and the State Department's exchange program is about $300 million. Over 4,000 Americans and almost 5,000 foreign nationals are employed in the program in the United States and overseas.

There are indications that American policy information efforts have decreased in emphasis since the U.S. Information Agency was created as a separate government agency in 1953. Policy advocacy was a vital activity of the State Department prior to 1953. With the functions now lodged in an independent agency, the direct connection between the policy-makers and the policy-advocates has been weakened. The State Department, which has the know-how to carry out this function, does not have the mandate and the manpower to do so; while USIA, which has the authority and manpower, does not have the direct access to policy it requires.

Nevertheless, USIA has a well-established operational system for handling this function. A teletyped wireless file goes to 130 monitoring stations five days a week carrying policy information material for ambassadors and mission personnel along with considerable amounts of cultural material (8,000-15,000 words daily). Particularly useful are transcripts of White House and State Department press briefings. USIS* officers overseas attempt, sometimes very successfully, to perform press attache functions. In some posts, USIS officers are requested by their ambassadors to report on political developments as they relate to informational activities.

As noted in Chapter II, the United States had only a small cultural communications program before the war. Therefore, American cultural communicators had to begin almost from scratch in 1945. Academic exchanges were given impetus with the inauguration of the Fulbright program. At the same time, information or cultural centers, including libraries, were established all over the world. Film programs and magazines specially produced for country or regional distribution followed suit. Soon these media became the vital tools of USIS officers who were stationed in American embassies and consulates in nearly every country in the world.

At the present time, USIA publishes nine periodicals abroad, while seven magazines are produced in Washington for worldwide or regional distribution. These 16 titles have a circulation of over 1,000,000. For purposes of comparison, *Time-Europe* has a weekly circulation of 1,370,000; *Newsweek International*, 442,000; and *Reader's Digest* over 30,000,000 in several language editions.

Most USIA films are acquired from the American private sector for showing abroad, and the agency only infrequently produces its own. The themes stressed are mainly tourism, science and technology, culture and the arts, and this year the Bicentennial.

The USIS libraries, found in almost all the 129 information centers around the world, originally were set up to provide material for enhancing knowledge of American society. They have now taken on a broadened variety of functions, serving as evidence of the vitality and richness of American life as shown in literary and scholarly creativity; a base of support for American studies program; and a vehicle for influencing the attitudes and opinions of political decision-makers and leaders of the communications media.

USIA exhibits, particular those shown in Eastern Europe, which have attracted hundreds of thousands of viewers, usually have a cultural, scientific, or technological theme.

In addition to these USIA cultural programs, the State Department's cultural program, carried out by the Bureau of Educational and Cultural

*USIS: United States Information Service.

Affairs, includes academic and nonacademic exchanges. Abroad, however, USIA officers administer the program, often in conjunction with binational commissions. It should be emphasized that the government handles only a fraction of the exchange activities—the great majority are sponsored by the private sector. The number of exchangees under State Department auspices in 1975 was slightly over 5,000. In addition to the academic exchangees (that is, professors and students) who usually remain overseas for a year or more, nonacademic exchangees, involving three- to six-week visits, come from the ranks of leaders in various professional fields such as politics, journalism, and the law.

Cultural presentations, such as the sending abroad of symphony orchestras, ballet groups, and artists, have been practically discontinued except in the Soviet Union and Eastern Europe, partly because of the cost factor and partly because the private sector has been active in such enterprises without governmental assistance.

USIA also operates the Voice of America, which broadcasts 784 hours weekly in 36 languages, including English, making the United States the biggest broadcaster of the five surveyed countries. VOA's annual budget is over \$60 million and the radio has 113 transmitters, 41 of them in the United States. The Voice of America operates under the following charter:

(1) VOA will extablish itself as a consistently reliable and authoritative source of news. VOA news will be accurate, objective, and comprehensive.

(2) VOA will represent America, not any single segment of American society. It will therefore present a balanced and comprehensive projection of significant American thought and institutions.

(3) As an official radio, VOA will present the policies of the United States clearly and effectively. VOA will also present responsible discussions and opinion on these policies.

This charter has recently been the subject of searching discussions both within the U.S. government and also in the U.S. Congress. The problem appears to be whether the mandate to broadcast "accurate, objective, and comprehensive news" is not in conflict with VOA's role as an "official" radio. American ambassadors have on several occasions complained that the broadcasting of certain news items, even if accurate, was injurious to U.S. foreign policy, and the State Department and USIA have generally backed them up.

The controversy is not easily settled. On the one hand, to omit a news item of significant importance not only contravenes the VOA charter but it is damaging to credibility, particularly if other international broadcasters (such as BBC and *Deutsche Welle*) carry the item. If that occurs, VOA inevitably loses listeners. On the other hand, to broadcast a news item that might harm the foreign relations of the United States understandably upsets the policy-maker and executor. And coming from an official U.S. government source the report may seem to have some color of official approval or sanction—and confuse listeners. Official condemnation, disavowal, or mitigation becomes "editorializing" and objectivity is lost.

Hence it is an inherent contradiction to have an "official" radio which carries "accurate, objective, and comprehensive" news. BBC and *Deutsche Welle* do not have the problem since they are not the "official" radio of Britain and the Federal Republic of Germany. Recent study commissions have recommended that the United States follow suit and set up VOA in such a manner as to make it less official, that is, to establish a buffer (for instance a governing board) between the policy-maker and the Voice.[5]

American policy information and cultural communications programs in the four countries surveyed mirror the importance attached by those countries to their American programs. The United States Information Agency puts Germany and Japan in its first resource allocation group, making them among the four most important countries for the United States. France is in group two, placing it with the top 12, while Britain is in group three and thus only among the top 30 of the 150-odd countries ranked. As Table 3 indicates, the resulting programs in Germany and Japan are very large indeed both in dollar terms and in personnel, far larger (especially in the case of Japan) than their programs in the United States. The programs in France and Britain are considerably smaller, and furthermore seem to be even smaller than the French and British programs here. Thus, the United States and the other four nations seem to share roughly similar conceptions of their importance to each other.

TABLE 3
American Information and Cultural Programs Overseas

	Resource Allocation Group	Funding FY 1975 $ in Thousands			Personnel		
		USIA	CU*	Total	U.S.	Local	Total
France	II	3,392	549	3,941	13	66	79
F.R.G.	I	5,088	2,555	8,643	29	118	147
U.K.	III	1,365	838	2,203	10	33	43
Japan	I	5,332	1,451	6,783	26	16	192

*Includes funds provided by host country.
Compiled from USIA Country Data papers, 1976 and CU sources.

In spite of the divided organizational structure in Washington, U.S. policy information and cultural communications are unified in the field. There the single organization known as the United States Information Service (USIS) is headed by a public affairs officer, who oversees both the cultural and information programs. The combination makes it extremely difficult to determine the balance between policy information and cultural communications. One can only rely on the estimates of public affairs officers who feel that the U.S. program is 80 to 90 percent cultural.

The American program in France is third in size among these four overseas programs. It is located almost entirely in Paris; there are no branch posts or information centers outside the capital, though five local employees represent USIS at American consulates in the provinces. USIS officials believe they are working in an improved atmosphere in France, where attitudes toward America (unlike those toward France prevalent in the United States according to French officials here) have improved rapidly since the advent of Giscard d'Estaing. The primary American objective in policy information there is to show Frenchmen that their country has more to gain from cooperation with the United States than from opposition to it— a message in some conflict with the French effort to persuade Americans that an independent ally is better than a subservient one. On the cultural side the Americans hope to encourage cooperation and a perception of interdependence of the two nations through a deeper French examination and understanding of American society.

All this is undertaken through media efforts and personal contacts. The press office maintains contact with the French press corps, serves as embassy spokesman and advises the ambassador on press relations, and reports to the rest of the embassy and to Washington on French press reactions. A press documentation center is maintained to give rapid background information on policy and "contemporary America," and a variety of press releases (including full texts of important speeches) are prepared for distribution. USIS also runs a small radio placement effort, which is principally successful among stations outside Paris. The American effort in television is expanding quite rapidly in France, with a considerable increase in the placement of U.S. films on French TV and heavy emphasis on facilitative assistance to French TV crews who are interested in coming to the United States to do reports for airing back home. There is also a small film lending library that makes about 4,000 loans each year.

Though much of the radio and video production cited above is cultural, the backbone of American cultural efforts in France is the American Cultural Center in the student quarter supplemented by the nearby Benjamin Franklin Reference Library. Here the seminars, lectures, exhibits, film programs, and other events that expose interested Parisians to American society are held. In the provinces, USIS works through universities and local centers of cultural activity, sending American scholars, artistic works, and performers for presentation. The human material for these efforts is provided in the main by the exchange program, which annually brings seven or eight Americans on short-term grants to France and includes a Fulbright academic program involving 40 Americans and 60 Frenchmen. It also sends about 30 French visitors for short stays in the U.S. Grant recipients are French political leaders and activists, economic policy makers, science and technology specialists, urban planners, and mass media specialists. The post also does a considerable amount of educational counseling for French students and others trying to find places as students or teachers in American educational institutions.

Substantial as this program is, it appears modest in comparison with the American effort in Germany. Partially a holdover from the massive postwar denazification program, this $8,500,000 program blankets the German nation and draws large resources from Germany itself. In 15 different cities outside the main post in Bonn, there are seven branch posts (defined as USIS offices with at least one American), seven jointly-funded German-American Institutes, and seven America Houses (wholly American-run and financed). The dispersal of the American program doubtless relates to the decentralized nature of postwar Germany, but in its totality it is nearly the largest single USIS program in the world. In its size and geographical breadth it corresponds well with the German program of Goethe Institutes in the United States, indicating that each country clearly treats the other as its most important ally.

On the whole, USIS officials believe that the German public is extremely favorable to the United States but not so blindly approving as it once was; today the West Germans are worried about threats of U.S. troop withdrawal and have begun to assert themselves more aggressively as leaders in Europe. Thus the two U.S. policy information objectives in Germany are to strengthen German understanding of American economic policies (including trade, monetary issues, energy, and resources) and to maintain German confidence in the American commitment to the Atlantic alliance. This last goal in particular nicely complements the German goal here of reminding the United States of its ally's importance—indeed, in contrast to the French case, the two countries' policy information goals seem mutually reinforcing. In cultural communications the United States hopes to show Germany that it is a creative and dynamic society that can produce solutions to common societal problems, to strengthen the capacity of German institutions to understand the interdependence of the United

States and Germany; and to enhance American understanding of German society and culture and its importance to America. Again, the goals of the American and German programs seem to be mutually reinforcing.

USIS personnel in Germany perform much the same functions as their counterparts in France, though on a broader scale. On the policy information side the press attache acts as embassy spokesman, writes ambassadorial speeches, maintains liaison with the Bonn press corps, and reports on German press reaction for the embassy and Washington. Texts of important American policy speeches and documents are distributed to academic, political, media, and other leaders, and the embassy has also undertaken a series of high-level background briefings for German media leaders with the ambassador. This policy-oriented work shades into cultural communications in the electronic media, where the post—paralleling the pattern in Paris—relies heavily on facilitative assistance to German TV crews seeking to do stories on the United States. Some placement of USIA television spots and VOA radio programs is accomplished, but radio has been so overshadowed by TV that the post produces no radio material locally at all. Videotape recording technology (VTR) has been used heavily as a part of library facilities in the field.

Most activities of the cultural program take place in these libraries and the America Houses in which they are located across Germany. USIS libraries in the Federal Republic are operated as an active service directed at selected audiences. In place of the usual mass circulation public library, they rely on a small reference collection, a thematically organized book collection, and an in-depth group of current periodicals supplemented by electronic nonprint sources (microform, VTR). The library then reaches out to its target audience, advertising its thematic concentrations and offering free distribution of the latest U.S. materials in the subject areas of their interest. The centers themselves are the locale for various lectures, seminars, conferences, and other events that fulfill thematic purposes; there is little in the way of performing arts or exhibits here, due to high cost and relatively low apparent effectiveness.

On the academic side, American cultural efforts have several areas of concentration. One is the teaching of English, done by the jointly-funded German-American institutes on a self-supporting basis through tuition charges. USIS provides pilot projects, teaching materials, and guidance. Another area of support is American studies programs in German schools and universities, where the U.S. effort is to teach the teachers of these subjects through exchanges, seminars, distribution of printed material, lecturers, curriculum development projects, and so forth. Educational counseling is also a vital function of the German effort as it is in France.

USIS also runs a sizable exchange program. In the short-term program there are about 35 German international visitors to the United States each year, and 10 Americans receive grants to visit Germany. The large Fulbright program receives well over half its funds from the Federal Republic; 450 people are exchanged under it, with the flow in each direction of roughly equal magnitude. Though the short-term exchange is thus slightly larger than France's, the academic side is four-and-a-half times larger—reflecting the generous support of the German government.

The U.S. effort in Britain is the smallest of the four programs and (like that in France) one exclusively centered in the capital city. The American program here operates in a historically favorable climate built on the "special relationship" between the two countries. Nevertheless, as in Germany, it is an atmosphere recently troubled by economic and political issues that USIS fears may provoke stereotypes of a rich, aggressive, and domineering America.

In this situation American policy information objectives are similar to those in the other European countries surveyed. They stress building appreciation for U.S. economic policies and their compatibility with British interests and promoting active support for continued cooperation between the two countries in security matters. In cultural communications the goals are to increase British confidence that American institutions can deal justly and effectively with social and political change and are innovative in responding to the challenge of post-industrial society; to increase respect for American cultural and intellectual achievements; and to broaden the number of people in each country who have a genuine understanding of the other's society and culture.

It is clear from even a cursory examination of American programs in Britain that there is nothing here like the imbalance between policy information and cultural communications that characterizes the British program in the United States. If anything, the United States' cultural effort is stronger than its policy advocacy in spite of the enormous private cultural flow between the two English-speaking countries. Policy information is also less closely tied than in France and Germany to the needs of the ambassador and seems to be centered on getting authoritative printed information to the British press. Distribution of policy-related material is accomplished through daily mini-cab delivery service to London's major newspapers, and through selected mailings to specialist writers and editors. The usual press conferences for U.S. officials are arranged and media reaction reporting is undertaken. The post is able to secure some placement of USIA films on national television, but does not operate a film lending service.

Almost from its inception USIS cultural communications in the United Kingdom have focused on the development of American studies; today, half its budget goes to support that objective, paralleling the British educational effort in the United States. In addition to that concern, the program concentrates on building contacts with and appreciation of American society and culture among selected audiences: members of parliament, labor and management leaders, academicians, media leaders, intellectuals and artists, and others influential in economic, social, and scientific policymaking. To accomplish these objectives the post runs a seminar series on American studies, sponsors over 125 lectures annually, and runs a modest reference library in the embassy. Though very few American professionals are brought to Britain for short visits on U.S. funding, the broad private flow provides sufficient talent to fuel these programs, and the post is able to send 15 to 20 Britons on short visits to America. There is also the Fulbright academic program, two-thirds funded by the United States, which brings about 50 Americans to Britain yearly and provides travel grants to almost 100 Britons. The small size of the USIS program means, however, that many of the activities counted on by other posts are not available in England. There is neither a book donation nor a cultural presentation program. More remarkable, there is not a single cultural center or binational institute, in sharp contrast to the dozen plus in Germany. And of course, there is no program to support English teaching. Like the British program in the United States, it is in many ways a modest effort.

American programs in Japan, though not quite on the order of those in Germany, are substantial and far more elaborate than anything the Japanese have in the United States. As in Germany, the scale is in part an inheritance from the postwar occupation period, but it also relates to the strategic and economic importance of Japan to the United States today. American officials in Japan assess public opinion there as showing much the same pattern as in Germany and England: generally favorably disposed toward America, yet threatened by economic pressures, domestic political uncertainty, and rising nationalism.

On the policy side, USIS objectives are to convince the Japanese that parallel and cooperative policies, especially in economic and security matters, will best serve the interests of Japan, and that the United States can be depended upon to back those interests. In cultural efforts the Americans hope to improve Japanese appreciation of American social and political institutions and of her creativity in the arts. These are objectives that fit well with the Japanese emphasis in the United States on the common features of Japanese and American societies.

The American policy information program in Japan relies heavily on press operations and on media relations liaison: writing the ambassador's speeches, monitoring Japanese media, holding press conferences for U.S. officials, distributing policy statements, and so forth. Work in the fast media is limited, however, by the super-saturated and highly advanced Japanese communications environment. There is, for example, no USIS film-lending program, and it is virtually impossible to place worthwhile material in meaningful time slots on Japanese TV. Radio is so uninfluential in Japan that USIS attempts neither placement nor facilitation. VTR is used, however, in the context of the six information and cultural centers.

It is here, in fact, that both American policy information and cultural communications are centered. USIS's effort to find an effective format in Japan's highly sophisticated communications environment has produced a concept called "Infomat;" it is the furthest development in American programs of the kind of active library facility being instituted in Germany. Infomats are specialized reference and research facilities, designed to meet the needs of a highly selective target audience, and providing the latest American materials not available elsewhere in Japan in five thematic areas: international affairs, economics, U.S. society, creative arts, and "the year 2000." The collection of books is small, up-to-date, and backed by the latest audio-visual technology. It is then advertised to individuals in the target audience selected through an elaborate biographical file. In addition, the centers each produce 40 to 50 programs a year in which many media forms and events over a two- or three-day period are tailored around a particular theme. The combination of Infomat and these packaged programs makes the American cultural communications effort in Japan among the most modern efforts of its kind in the world.

USIS-Japan also makes use of the traditional slower media, which still seem quite applicable in the Japanese environment. The post produces a bi-monthly quality magazine in Japanese that supports program themes, and it distributes copies of USIA-produced worldwide periodicals. It tries to stimulate the translation of important American books on matters related to the mission's objectives by making publishers aware of them and occasionally providing financial support. The exchange-of-persons program is modest compared to Germany's, probably because of language difficulty, but it is also quite different in being proportionally far more concentrated on the nonacademic short-term grant for professionals in politics, government, media, universities, and the arts. Almost 70 international visitors come to the United States yearly from Japan for 30-day visits, and about 15 American specialists go in the other direction. The academic program includes 80-odd Fulbright grantees, two-thirds of them Japanese coming to America.

IV. POLICY INFORMATION AND CULTURAL COMMUNICATIONS—TWO DIFFERENT FOREIGN POLICY FUNCTIONS

Our survey has confirmed what history and logic seemed to show. The information and cultural programs of the major Western industrial countries, sometimes grouped under the title "public diplomacy," really form two quite different functions. One is a policy information effort, which has as its purpose the articulation and defense of the nation's foreign policy overseas and generally operates as a part of the political section of the foreign ministry and embassy. The other function is cultural communications, designed to portray the national society abroad and managed either by a separate cultural section of the foreign ministry and embassy or by an entity all but independent of the government itself (such as, Alliance Française, Goethe Institute, British Council, and Japan Foundation). With the single exception of the U.S. government, this is in fact the way the programs are run, both at home and overseas.

It is clear that the concern of Western governments to separate policy information from culture springs directly from their emphasis on the portrayal of their societies overseas and their feeling that this task is at least equal to any short-term gain that might be acquired from more energetic advocacy of a particular foreign policy. This belief in turn often relates to the separateness, the duality of public and private life in their view—their conviction that there is a private society and culture to represent abroad, and that the value of the nation is uniquely to be found there. Along with this belief generally goes a distrust of governments, which in the parliamentary tradition are seen to be ephemeral and merely tolerated as necessary for the political governance of the nation. Thus it is no accident that France, with its strong emphasis on cultural excellence and its history of governmental instability, should possess the most divided program. Nor is it suprising that in the United States, where the information and cultural efforts resulted directly from the Second World War and the subsequent Cold War, policy information and cultural communications still appear in a more unified form.

Of course, the reasons for separating policy information from cultural communications are practical as well as philosophical and appear in these programs at every level, from the objectives they serve to the messages they carry to the media they use. Policy information is a highly political function, moving from issue to issue on a day-to-day basis with the foreign policy of the government in power. Cultural communications is a long-range effort representing the nation (rather than the government) in all its stability and character. Policy information must advocate and defend; it is by nature partisan and biased. Cultural communications explains and portrays; it must give at least the impression of truthfulness in order to be credible and effective. Policy information uses the fast media, such as radio, TV, and the press. Cultural communications needs the slower books, exhibits, and films that provide the kind of visual and in-depth verbal treatment cultural subjects require. The source of policy information is of course the government, whereas the most authentic cultural materials come from the private sector they seek to portray.

As the surveyed programs show, these differences demand separate organizations placed in different proximity to the foreign policy apparatus. The policy information function requires the closest connection with foreign office policy-makers so that the spokesman will possess the knowledge about policy necessary to successful articulation and defense of it. Indeed, since only the policy-maker himself could reasonably be expected to have such knowledge, and since the top spokesmen are always the top policy-makers anyway (namely, the foreign minister, his deputies, and key ambassadors), it is hard to imagine the spokesman role being carried out effectively by anybody except the policy-makers themselves and their press assistants. Association of the cultural communications program with the policy-makers, on the other hand, could only be detrimental to each. Portrayal of a society abroad is a highly operational, long-range program that would distract the policy-maker from his day-to-day concerns. It involves the management and orchestration of a variety of media for which he has no time, and it should be run free of political pressures inherent in the policy process that might compromise its credibility and thereby damage its effectiveness. With good reason to avoid contact with the policy-maker, the cultural program has need instead of intensive relationships with the private sector whence it secures source material and media products. These relationships, too, are more easily formed by an organization placed at some distance from the foreign policy bureaucracy.

It is clear, then, that if policy information and cultural communications are unified, some of the conditions requisite to the successful operation of one or both may not be met. The spokesmen may be too far removed from the policy information they are supposed to disseminate and their work then becomes irrelevant, as is the case with the United States today. Or the cultural program may be too politicized and thus lose much of its credibility, as is the case with the Soviet Union, and during some recent periods with the United States. Indeed, it appears that the creation of a separate Information Agency in the United States and the splitting of the cultural program between USIA and the State Department may have resulted in the worst of all possible worlds—removing the spokesman role from the policy-maker and politicizing cultural communications.

The near-universal separation of policy information and cultural communications is paralleled by the striking similarity of all eight policy information programs surveyed. Numbers of personnel are roughly comparable and the functions are virtually the same, be it Japan's program in the United States or the American program in France. In the industralized countries, the fast media on which an outgoing policy information program must depend are almost useless due to saturation of the communications environment: TV and press placement are impossible, and no one listens to shortwave radio. Hence, policy information becomes essentially a press and media relations effort, in which officers deal informally with host media personnel in a constant effort to keep them on the right track.

The policy information programs we have surveyed are also characterized by what might at first seem a striking harmony for programs advocating foreign policy issues. The calm doubtless reflects the relatively good political relations among the allies at the time our survey took place. Only between the United States and France was there lingering discord, and only here were the fundamental objectives of the policy information program at odds (over whether the lesser ally should be subservient to or independent of the greater).

This is not to imply that policy information is not important; indeed, it is used by all the junior partners of the United States to gain some additional leverage over their giant ally And in more general terms it is clear that in today's world every country has to have a policy information program because the policies of each government—even the smallest—have to be explained. Often presidents, prime ministers, foreign ministers, and ambassadors are the primary or only spokesmen. But as countries increase in political importance, larger policy information establishments become necessary and separate press spokesmen are established at home and at embassies overseas. Hence the sizable apparatus we see conducting these relationships in Washington, Paris, Bonn, London, and Tokyo today.

If the similarities are most obvious in policy information, it is the differences that strike one among the surveyed programs in cultural communications. Just compare the American program in Britain with that in Germany or Japan, or the German and British programs in the United States with each other! Beyond the vast differences in size and level of resources devoted to cultural communications, which tend to vary with the relationship between the receiving and the sending country, there is a basic difference in character between the American programs surveyed and those of the other industrialized countries. The cultural communications efforts of France, Germany, the United Kingdom, and Japan seem to be largely passive, designed to distribute factual material about the foreign society in the United States but not to push specific themes with the purpose of correcting mistaken American views or building a favorable image where none existed. In contrast, the Americans tend to see cultural communications as providing the context within which policy advocacy can be effective. This in turn leads to a more activist style for American cultural communications, based on the idea that foreign peoples have certain misconceptions about the United States that must be corrected and that the American program should be an outgoing thematically-oriented one designed to instill a particular image of America in the minds of the target audience.

It is of course possible to overstate the differences here. The basic task of all cultural programs, to build intersocietal understanding, usually leads to objectives that are mutually reinforcing, as was amply demonstrated by the reciprocal programs surveyed. Moreover, a large proportion of American as well as foreign programs are consciously nonthematic; that is, designed simply to present overseas a picture of the national life and thought that will be seen as worthy of respect. The particulars may change according to differing national identities, but all those surveyed wish to be seen as economically advanced, socially and politically progressive nations, which desire a peaceful world and friendly relations with all other states, and which bear a special concern for and ability to relate to developing countries. Beyond this common core are differences arising out of regional and political positions or particular economic goals (for example, the

British and Japanese situations). The cultural images are different, but the responses they seek to evoke are the same and so they are cast in similar form. Even the media used are basically the same. The cynical might call this homogeneity the inevitable result of propaganda; the optimist might find here impressive and unexpected evidence of the extent to which we are already, beneath our competitive instincts, one world.

Perhaps the most intriguing question in all of this is why nations undertake the expensive effort to display their national character abroad in the first place. Every nation must defend its foreign policy, but why cultural communications?

Among the strongest motivations are those that spring from the concept of national identity and the need to assert it. Nations, like men, tend to see themselves through the eyes of others, and many feel a need to manifest the national character abroad almost as part of the process of defining it at home. The French, for example, engage in cultural communications because representing the eternal values of *la patrie* overseas is simply one of the things great nations do—and the French think of themselves as a great nation. The Germans turned to cultural communications after World War II as a necessary part of recreating the national image after the Nazi debacle. This kind of motivation is so powerful not only because it springs from the deep sources of nationalism but also because it demands no justification by results. The doing is sufficient to the ends sought.

Many nations, of course, undertake cultural programs precisely for the results they are expected to produce. In several cases these results are highly specific: the British hope to increase sales abroad, the Japanese want to stimulate tourism to Japan, and so forth. Some nations even profess a desire for internal payoffs—a hope, for example, that exchange of professionals in the fields of crime prevention and environmental pollution will lead to a crime-free America and clearer Japanese air. There might even be political goals in view, as when the United States tries to explain its internal politics and domestic political system to foreign peoples in order to assure them that in spite of all appearances the United States is a dependable society whose friendship can be trusted. Cultural communications can in these ways be tied to very specific national goals.

Cultural communications are often undertaken to support foreign policy in a more general way than that described above. Many nations believe that a cultural program is necessary as a background for foreign policy, that a degree of cultural understanding is needed before nations of dissimilar cultural heritage can communicate with each other. Cultural communications thus supports foreign policy by helping to provide the background of mutual understanding needed for the communication of policy goals and ideas. It also supports the diplomacy of smaller nations vis-à-vis bigger ones by keeping the former visible in the home territory of the latter. This is a motivation pointed to by most of those operating these programs in the United States today.

Finally, and without evidence to the contrary one must take their word for it, some nations undertake cultural programs in the interest of world peace. Doubtless they conceive the peace in terms favoring their interests, but the preservation of peace is certainly in the interest of most nations today. The argument here is an old one, to the effect that war will cease only when the peoples of the world understand each other well enough to respect differing views and avoid the passionate hatreds that block solutions of disputes between them. There are, of course, differences between states that cannot be resolved by reason, and wars have occurred between states who understand each other perfectly. But because an argument cannot be proven right does not mean it is certainly wrong. We should not allow the cynicism of our times to stand in the way of a great ideal whose time yet may come, particularly when the stakes are so very high.

In the 1950s it was customary to speak of propaganda in terms of a great struggle for men's minds, of campaigns of truth and psychological warfare. On the urgent battlefields of the cold war the defense and promulgation of such cultural values as democracy, individual freedom, and enterprise became a part of American foreign policy as the Western world girded itself to resist the onslaughts of a powerful adversary. Today, in the 1970s and in the context of relations between Western allies, policy information and cultural communications programs play a radically different role. What we have surveyed are rather gentlemanly and low-keyed efforts, carefully designed to support and knit still closer the ties of economic and politico-security alliances while at the same time providing a means for each country to further its own interests within the boundaries of the common relationship. In this context cultural relations are no longer part of the battleground whereon foreign policy differences are fought. Instead they form the background and, through the development of mutual understanding, may one day form the common ground on which may be sought the reconciliation of those differences.

NOTES

1. This chapter is particularly indebted to Part I of Haigh (1974).

2. In the following program summaries, the authors have found especially helpful the data on worldwide program emphasis and organization in the capitals provided in the USIA series on External Information and Cultural Relations Programs, produced by the USIA Office of Research and Assessment, Washington, D.C., as follows: *France,* 1973; *Federal Republic of Germany,* 1973; *United Kingdom,* 1973; *Japan,* 1973.

3. The New York service was created by de Gaulle's Free French to lobby their cause during World War II, in an era when Vichy representatives were in Washington and the center of press activity in the United States was New York. It was strengthened in the mid-1950s to counter Arab propaganda at the UN during the Algerian war.

4. The center was established in New York during the early 1960s to take information work off the hands of the embassy, on the theory that New York is the headquarters of the news industry in the U.S. and out of concern for good relationships with the American Jewish community. Today this rationale seems less compelling, and it is possible that the center will soon be moved back to Washington.

5. For a complete exposition of the problems faced by Western international shortwave broadcasters, see Abshire (1976).

REFERENCES

ABSHIRE, D. M. (1976) International Broadcasting: A New Dimension of Western Diplomacy. The Washington Papers, 35, Center for Strategic and International Studies. Beverly Hills and London: Sage Publications.

Commission on the Organization of the Government for the Conduct of Foreign Policy (1975) Robert D. Murphy, chairman. Report. Washington: U.S. Gov. Print. Office.

Congressional Research Service (1975) The United States Communicates with the World: A Study of U.S. International Information and Cultural Programs and Activities. Washington: Library of Congress.

HAIGH, A. (1974) Cultural Diplomacy in Europe. Strasbourg: Council of Europe.

JAMES, W. (1955) Pragmatism. Cleveland: World Pub.

Panel on International Information, Education, and Cultural Relations (1975) Recommendations for the Future. Washington: Center for Strategic and International Studies.

Washington Post (1976) "Tokyo front lobbies covertly in U.S." (September 15).